ADAM WAS A PUNK!

And Other Lessons From Scripture

By R.M. Green

Safe Haven Publishing Company

SAFE HAVEN PUBLISHING COMPANY
P.O. BOX 4673
BEAUFORT, SOUTH CAROLINA 29903

ISBN: 978-0615835099

United States Copyright Office
101 Independence Avenue SE
Washington, DC 20559-6000

FIRST EDITION

FIRST PRINTING

THE CHAIR

My soul just yearned and screamed,

Reaching out to find someone who cared

Then I opened my eyes, and it seemed

The only thing that heard was that empty chair.

When I realised that I was all alone

Tears rolled from my heart through my eyes

There was no need to talk on the phone

When all I heard was death and lies.

Deep down inside I felt there was no hope

All that awaited was pain and despair,

Until I felt that wind blow past my earlobe

And that raindrop caressed my cheek, resting there.

I knew then that someone heard my cry,

Came to lift my spirits and brought me joy.

I turned my head and searched the sky

To see His face, and feel His presence to enjoy.

He made the sun come out and shine again,

Made the birds sing, the flowers bloom on the stair.

He heard my screams, and He cared then,

For Jesus was the One sitting in that Chair.

~TABLE OF CONTENTS~

FOREWORD

First off, I'd like to start off by saying that I am no one special. By that, I mean I hold no special title of Preacher, Evangelist, Reverend, Bishop, Prophetess, Apostle, etc. I am just a woman, a mother of three beautiful daughters and a new grandmother, with a heart for God, who wishes to tell others the Good News of eternal salvation through our Lord Jesus Christ.

I have been a believer in Jesus Christ all my life, but throughout all the years I have been going (and admittedly, NOT going) to church, I still had many questions in the back of my mind that needed answers. I needed these answers to fully grasp and embrace my true understanding of who God is, who Jesus Christ is, why we do so many things the way we do when we are in church, and how these answers would affect my life. After receiving the answers to these questions, and finally gaining more understanding by reading and studying the Bible, and scripture lessons from pastors who know and believe the Bible is the true and complete Word of God, one thing became dreadfully clear – I was a carnal Christian.

I believed, and I could talk the talk – but I was DEFINITELY not walking the walk. I had to learn to build a relationship with God; read and study His Word (*"Be diligent to present yourself approved to God a worker who does not need to be ashamed, rightly dividing the word of truth." - 2 Timothy 2:15*), attend church and fellowship with like minded Christians (*"Not forsaking our own assembling together, as is the habit of some, but encouraging one another; and all the more as you see the day drawing near." - Hebrews 10:25*), pray and fast *(And He said to them, 'This cannot come about by anything but prayer and fasting'." - Mark 9:29)*, but most importantly – to TRUST GOD (*"And my God will supply all your needs according to His riches in glory in Christ Jesus." - Philippians 4:19*). I I had to give my life over to Him, and stop behaving, thinking and LOOKING like the world, and live my life as God would have me live it, in honor and praise to Him - mind, body and soul.

On December 16, 2007, I seriously accepted Jesus Christ into my life, and vowed that I would live it for Him, according to His will and His way as described in the Bible. This meant no more conforming to the world, but I had to conform to Christ, and trust Him in ALL things; no more fornication or sex outside of marriage (no more 'booty-calls' or 'friends with benefits', and no sex on dates); less exposure to media or 'reality TV', sex & dating shows; even down to believing horoscopes, psychics, gossiping, cutting out some music, alcoholic drinks... and that's just the beginning of things. His Word will also teach you how to handle money, business, relationships, and problems as they arise – you simply have to know what God says about an issue, then trust Him and apply it; doing this has made my life much easier on many occasions, and avoided other pitfalls during the storms of life as they occurred. It is a process I am still going through, to renew my mind and point it toward Christ at all times, and have my body follow; however it is a process one naturally goes through when one truly seeks to get closer to Christ and live their life for Him. It is not easy, as I find myself in conflict with many of today's socially-accepted behaviors and thought patterns, but I continue to strive because I seek to do His will! *"Seek FIRST the kingdom of God and His righteousness; and all these things shall be added unto you."* - *Matthew 6:33*. That is when He shall give you life right here on earth, more abundantly, and receive the desires of your heart. Also, when my life is over, when it is all said and done, I want to hear the words, "Well done, my good and faithful servant!"when He receives me on Judgment Day.

In actuality, even though I do not hold any sort of official title, God's Word says, *"But you are a chosen people, a royal priesthood, a Holy nation, a people for God's own possession, so that you may proclaim the excellencies of Him who has called you out of darkness into His marvelous light;"* - *1 Peter 2:9*. And we are all called as Christians to be Ministers to all people, to fulfill God's Great Commission, as He commands us to *"Go therefore and make disciples of all the nations, baptizing them in the name of the Father, and the Son and the Holy Spirit, teaching them to observe all that I commanded you; and lo, I am with you always, even to the end of the age."* - *Matthew 28:19-20*.

This is the purpose of me putting this book together, not only to minister to His people, but that maybe my words can bring about an understanding to some that would spark a thirst for more of God's word, and a closer relationship with Him, and to go out and make disciples for Him. Physically, I am limited to share His word with others by where I happen to be located at the time, only to those around me, or by those who know me and can reach me physically or by phone. However, with this book, I pray that I am able to reach at least one more person and share the Good News with them and bring them to Christ, or at least bring them closer to an understanding of my relationship with Him, and how they can have a personal relationship with Him as well.

As I close this note, all I can say is that these are a collection of my poems and lessons I have learned from my studies and teachings; I advise that you look up these verses, attend a Bible-teaching, Bible believing church and study them for YOURSELVES, under the teaching of your own pastors and show yourselves approved, and form your own relationship with God. In Revelations 3:20, Jesus says, *"Behold, I stand at the door and knock; if anyone hears My voice and opens the door, I will come in to him and will dine with him, and he with Me."* Once you let Him into your heart and your life, He promises, *"I will never leave you nor forsake you,"* *Hebrews 13:5.*

May God continue to bless you and keep you.

Peace & Blessings,
R.M. Green

P.S.: I would like to acknowledge the following pastors of sound Christian doctrine: Pastor Benjamin Glover, Grace and Truth Gospel Chapel, St. Helena SC; Pastor Carl Broggi, Community Bible Church, Beaufort SC; Pastor Tony Evans, Oak Cliff Bible Fellowship, Dallas TX; Dr. Charles Stanley, Founder & President of In Touch Ministries and Senior Pastor of First Baptist Church in Atlanta, Georgia; and Pastor John F. MacArthur, Founder of radio ministry Grace To You Ministries, Los Angeles, CA.

HOW GRATEFUL ARE YOU TO GOD?

"As He entered a village, ten leprous men who stood at a distance met Him; and they raised their voices, saying, "Jesus, Master, have mercy on us!" When He saw them, He said to them, 'Go and show yourselves to the priests.' And as they were going, they were cleansed. Now one of them, when he saw that he had been healed, turned back, glorifying God with a loud voice, and he fell on his face at His feet, giving thanks to Him. And he was a Samaritan." Luke 17:12-16.

The story above teaches us through Christ several lessons He wants us to learn. The first is of FAITH and OBEDIENCE. In that time, lepers lived in colonies separate from the regular population so that they would not spread their disease to others. They were shunned because it was thought that their sins were responsible for their condition, as the disease ate away at their flesh. The 10 lepers knew that Jesus was powerful enough and able to cure them if it was His will - so they called out to Him, and pleaded for His mercy. That was their first act of faith. Jesus saw them and He held compassion for them. When He instructed them to **"GO AND SHOW YOURSELVES TO THE PRIESTS"**, He knew that the only way they could leave that colony was to have a priest declare them cured, or 'clean'. As they went, AS THEY OBEYED Him, they were healed. They were not healed immediately, they had to ACT on His word, and be OBEDIENT to receive the blessing. All were obedient, and ALL became healed.

The next lesson is of GRATITUDE. Only ONE man came back to thank Him for his healing, and it was the Samaritan. As a Samaritan, he was usually thought of as an ENEMY of the Jews, and the other nine lepers were Jews. This Samaritan was the ONLY ONE grateful enough to come back and thank Him for His blessing! Even though He already knew how many would return, it breaks Jesus' heart whenever He blesses us and we don't return a proper 'Thank You' to Him. Yet, through His mercy and goodness, He healed ALL TEN men. The next few verses Jesus shows His disappointment that His own never thanked Him. ***"Then Jesus answered and said, 'Were there not ten cleansed? But the nine - where are they? Was no one found who returned to give glory to God, except this foreigner?' And He said to him, 'Stand up and go; your faith has made you well.'"*** ***Luke 17:17-19.*** It is Jesus Who deserved the Glory! The men did NOT heal themselves, He did! Even as the Samaritan was NOT a Jew, it was his **FAITH**, **OBEDIENCE** and **GRATITUDE** that made him well, and he was the **ONLY** one that gave God his glory!

Unfortunately, in real life, this represents how good and merciful God is with His blessings, even when we are NOT grateful to Him. We tend to pray and ask for things, and when we get them, do we truly thank Him? How much more do you think He will be ready to bless us if He knew we would always be grateful to Him, and give Him His glory? Did He wake you up this morning? Did you have food for your stomach, clothes on your back? Do you still have breath in your body? Are you READING THIS? Tomorrow is NOT promised, and we indeed need to thank Him for every moment of life given to us, because we can be snuffed out any second! Try to go an ENTIRE DAY, 24 hours, simply praying and THANKING the Lord - NOT ASKING for ANYTHING for yourself, just pray and THANK HIM, praise Him and give Him His glory - NOTHING ELSE. When you do this, you will see how HARD it is to pray and NOT ASK for something for yourself. It will show how selfish we really are, as well as teach us how BLESSED we really are, and what a loving and mighty God we serve!

Thank You, Dear JESUS - for each and every moment you allow us on this earth, and each and every blessing you bestow upon us all. In Jesus' Precious Name, I pray... AMEN!!

TREADING WATER

Smiling faces and hearty laughter
Can hide empty souls behind lying eyes;
Celebrations planned simply don't matter
When the heart is cold and void inside.

Sitting comfortably in a crowded room
Bustling with activity, beloveds and cheer,
Sometimes masks a feeling of impending doom
Mixed with anxiety, pain and fear.

Why do these clouds hang over the afflicted,
Moving at a standstill, trying to please the others?
Working like a fiend, as if addicted,
But living life just treading water?

Striving to be first, but ending up last,
Progress finally seeming within reach;
Breakthrough looming with expectations vast,
However this existence has other lessons to teach.

No matter what is done or said
It all seems to no avail.

With closed eyes and the bow of the head,

A prayer is sent up to God, asking Him to prevail.

'Nothing is too hard for God!'

The Bible does proclaim,

He will use one's enemies as their footstool,

Use their own weapons to put them to shame.

Jesus can turn all darkness to light,

Depression and gloom washed away by the Living Water!

Love and honor Him with all your soul and might,

No longer will one have to live life just...

Treading Water.

DO YOU TAKE ADVANTAGE OF GOD? DO YOU TAKE HIM FOR GRANTED?

"For sin shall not have dominion over you, for you are not under law but under grace." Romans 6:14.

Unfortunately, most of us DO take advantage of God, because they KNOW that if they commit a sin and ask forgiveness, He is faithful to forgive. This verse is often cited as a justification or license to sin, but the next verses in the Bible CLEARLY warns against such thinking: *"What then, Shall we sin because we are not under law, but under grace? CERTAINLY NOT! Do you not know that to whom you present yourselves slaves to obey, you are that one's slaves whom you obey, whether of sin leading to death, or of obedience leading to righteousness?" Romans 6:15-16.* This is the part of scripture that no one likes to talk about, because it makes us accountable for our actions before God. When you KNOWINGLY sin, you are consciously making a choice to reject God - and that makes you a slave to satan. We are either totally sold out to God or satan at any given time by our actions; there IS no in-between.

No matter how hard we try, we ARE going to stumble and sin, and fall short of the glory of God - even the Apostle Paul had that struggle. But it is always the INTENT OF THE HEART that God reads. It is one thing to, let's say, try to quit drinking, using drugs or quit smoking, but being in the midst of that struggle you may break down and take a puff or two, or pop a pill, take a drink - but once you do it, you ask God's forgiveness, try in earnest to get back on the wagon, get into a program or use other therapies to try and stop, God can forgive because He sees your struggles, and His grace is there to give you time to get it right. It is quite another to go out with the INTENTION of drinking, smoking, having sex, using drugs, stealing, lying, etc., thinking that all I have to is ask forgiveness, and He will forgive your sins. Your INTENT all along was to sin, and you can't hide from God behind that; He reads the intent of the HEART!

Just as one may mistreat another human being, thinking they will forgive them every time (like the spouse who cheats) until one day, the faithful spouse gets fed up and files for divorce, God ALSO has a time limit on repeated WILLFUL sinning - and you never know WHEN that time limit will be up - then He takes His hands off you, and leaves you to a reprobate mind, when you will be declared as satan's slave; *"And even as they did not like to retain God in their knowledge, God gave them over to a debased (or reprobate) mind to do those things which are not fitting; being filled with all unrighteousness, sexual immorality, wickedness, covetousness, maliciousness, full of envy, murder, strife, deceit, evil-mindedness; they are whisperers, backbiters, haters of God, violent, proud, boasters, inventors of evil things, disobedient to parents, undiscerning, untrustworthy, unloving, unforgiving, unmerciful; who, knowing the righteous judgment of God, that those who practice such things are deserving of death, not only do the same but also approve of those who practice them." Romans 1:28-31.*

In your walk with Christ, be sure you are holding on to His hand, because 'doing what YOU want to do' may just cost you your own salvation if you are NOT careful. Don't take advantage of God's kindness and goodness toward you, but use His grace to get it right, and hear 'Well done, my good and faithful servant!" when you meet Him on Judgment Day! **Amen and Hallelujah... Thank You Jesus!**

MY PASSION WITHIN

My passion within
Grows for you with each passing hour
Seeking to fulfill your wildest dreams,
Your deepest desires my mission to devour

My heart has been caged so long
Yearning to reach out and touch
The one who holds the ultimate key
To all that I am, whom I yearn for so much

I don't know what to say
Nor am I sure of what to do
The magic of that moment seems so close
But also so far away, the day I will finally taste you...

I must admit that I'm constantly in a battle
Do I please my flesh or God, this spiritual warfare
You know my body craves you more each day
But the love of my God carries greater care.

This I must say to you, my dearest,
That when I give of myself it is forever
Don't you see that I care for you so much
I want to protect your soul, so fire will not destroy it ever?

Can't you see that if I can deprive myself of you
The only man I truly crave more and more each day
Once we are together as one, no other will ever touch
That which belongs to you, whom I love in every way?

It is simply not enough to love the man
To whom I pledge my life to be my head
But to love Christ, Who shall always be front and center
Whom we both shall obey, follow Him and be lovingly led..

RUTH AND BOAZ: ARE YOU REALLY READY FOR LOVE?

Today, it is extremely difficult to be single and also be a faithful Christian. Especially when we see what the media bombards us, and our children, with on a constant basis – images of adultery, fornication, homosexuality, lying, cheating, murder, etc. in many of our favorite television shows, magazines, music, etc. It can seem like no one is paying attention to – or even caring – what God's Word has to say in all these situations. But as Christians, we have to live in this world, and try to honor God with our minds, our hearts and our bodies – and I hope this essay will give us some hope and strength to do just that. I draw my strength from the story of Naomi, Ruth and Boaz (Book of Ruth) and Proverbs 31, which tells of the characteristics of a Noble Wife.

But first, to understand where I was, to where living under the word of God has taken me, I must admit that I was once very much OUT THERE. I am going to bare my soul here. I thought that because I loved my boyfriend, that God would forgive me of the sins of fornication, living together without the benefit of marriage, reasoning that times have changed, and since God knows that, He will forgive and bless me because EVERYONE is doing it. I had been married, but prior to that I was in several long-term relationships, but when they ended I still continued seeing them as 'friends with benefits', because I had a 'need' that had to be satiated, and they did too. I also had been involved in an abusive relationship, and at one time even sold sex toys and lingerie to help make ends meet. Truthfully speaking, I loved sex, had a very strong drive and could not even fathom my life without it, no matter how it came, not to mention other sins. However, society said I wasn't a bad person, and I went along with life in the fast lane, and being quite comfortable in that life – for awhile.

Until one day it became very clear I was getting NOWHERE living this way. I found myself alone, divorced, with three children to raise – and very empty inside. What was I missing? What was I going to do to fill that huge – and widening – void in my life? Jesus Christ was the *ANSWER*!

On the invitation of a friend of mine (now my Pastor's wife) and a cousin, on a clear day in August, 2007, I attended a sermon at what would become my church home, and it changed my life. I continued to attend, and learned more about Who God really is, and what He could do for my life if I would just surrender it to Him – and on December 16, 2007, I did just that. I surrendered my life to Him and His will, and my life has become all the more rich and full for it. PRAISE AND GLORY BE TO GOD!

I now consider myself a 'Ruth', waiting on my 'Boaz' to redeem me. God had a LOT of work to do on me to get me to this point, and I know He is still working on me, but as I go on living my life to honor Him more and more, I know He will present me with the man He has for me, in His time. But I must live my life for Him in order for Him to deliver the desires of my heart – to be married and live happily ever after. *"Seek FIRST the kingdom of God and His righteousness, and all these things shall be added unto you."* Matthew 6:33.

I first had to tackle the truth that GOD DOES NOT CHANGE (**Malachi 3:6; James 1:17 and Numbers 23:19**). That means that WE must conform to HIS ways and His will, He does NOT conform to ours! So my former reasoning was indeed flawed, to say the least; it was dead WRONG! We have to renew our minds and not let this WORLD dictate our actions, thoughts and emotions.

What inspires me about Ruth's story is that God had made a way for not only her to be redeemed and find love again, but after Naomi (her mother-in-law) had lost both her sons and her husband, God had redeemed her too, out of Ruth's faith, obedience, loyalty and love for NAOMI and HER God, YHWH.

As explained in the Book of Ruth in our Holy Bible, Naomi and Elimelech (her husband), who were from Bethlehem in Judah, had taken up residence in Moab with their family, sons Mahlon and Kilion, where the Moabites had their own customs and gods they worshiped in their land. Their sons had taken two Moabite women, Ruth and Orpah, for their wives. Eventually Elimelech, Mahlon and Kilion were all killed, leaving all three women widows.

With her family gone, Naomi prepares to return to Bethlehem and bids her daughters-in-law goodbye, but Ruth refuses to stay with her people and declares, ***"Where you go I will go, and where you stay I will stay. Your people will be my people, and your God will be my God. Where you die I will die and there I will be buried. May the Lord deal with me, be it ever so severely, if anything but death separates you and me."*** Ruth 1:16-17. Her loyalty and dedication to Ruth indicates not only her love for and loyalty to Naomi, who according to Jewish custom is reduced to living in abject poverty since she too old to marry or have children to care for her, but also to God, Who saw this and was pleased. It is an early indication that as long as one believes in and obeys God's will and worships Him, one does NOT have to be born of Hebrew descent to receive His blessings!

Now Ruth went out to the fields of Boaz, a relative of Elimelech, to pick up the scraps of harvested barley that is left behind from the workers so that she and Naomi can eat. Boaz, who has heard by now of the loyalty and kindness of Ruth toward Naomi, became smitten with her, told her not to go anywhere else to gather food. Not only did he tell her that she is welcome there and to follow his servant girls, Boaz told the men to intentionally leave behind grain for her to pick up so she and Naomi can eat. Naomi, knowing that Boaz is a kinsman-redeemer (a relative who could marry and provide security for a widow), instructed Ruth, ***"Wash and perfume yourself and put on your best clothes. Then go down to the threshing floor, but don't let him know you are there until he has finished eating and drinking. When he lies down, note the place where he is lying. Then go and uncover his feet and lie down. He will tell you what to do."*** Ruth 3:3-4.

She obeyed and did as Naomi instructed, then stated to Boaz in verse 9, ***"Spread the corner of your garment over me, since you are a kinsman-redeemer."***

Boaz was impressed, and Ruth showed she was a woman of noble standing, verses 10-14; *"This kindness is greater than that which you showed earlier; you have not run after the younger men, whether rich or poor. And now, my daughter, don't be afraid. I will do for you all you ask. All my fellow townsmen know that you are a woman of noble character. Although it is true that I am near of kin, there is a kinsman-redeemer nearer than I. Stay here for the night, and in the morning if he wants to redeem, good, let him redeem. But if he is not willing, as surely as the Lord lives I will do it."*

Again, Ruth's obedience and loyalty to Naomi, her customs and her God, further led to eventual marriage of Ruth to Boaz. After he made sure that a closer relative would not do it, Boaz took Ruth for his own wife and, according to Hebrew laws, redeemed both Ruth and Naomi, since they would now both be well cared for by Boaz. They did everything right, and they did it God's way!

This story gives me inspiration to continue on my path to finally receive my Boaz, but I also want to be PREPARED to be a proper wife once God blesses me with him. For that I turn to Proverbs 31, which spells out how to be a Wife of Noble Character who is worth *"far more than rubies"* (verse 10). I especially take note of verses 11-12, *"Her husband has full confidence in her and lacks nothing of value. She brings him good, not harm, all the days of her life,"* and verses 23, *"Her husband is respected at the city gate, where he takes his seat among the elders of the land,"* and 30, *"Charm is deceptive, and beauty is fleeting, but a woman who fears the Lord is to be praised"*. ALL of Proverbs 31 is important, but I think these verses really sum it up for me, and how I should conduct myself, even BEFORE becoming a wife. God had to let me know what is expected of a Godly wife and put it into practice beforehand, so that once he blesses me with my husband, I will be ready and know how to properly praise Him by knowing how to care for a husband, our family and myself.

Now, what lessons have I learned by studying the Scriptures, and how do I apply them to my life? There are many to be sure, but here are some basic truths that I have learned and strive to live by:

1.   **HONOR GOD WITH MY BODY:** That means in ALL aspects – keeping it clean, well groomed, and REFRAIN from sex outside of marriage. The sex was a BIGGIE for me! To think that if I never get married, I would never have sex again was a REAL stretch for me – but now I have grown beyond that. One thing I know is that I love God enough to give up the ONE thing I found hardest to give up – and He has kept His promise that He would never leave me nor forsake me, and my life is much richer for this VERY reason. Now that sex, and the emotional ties that go along with it, are not in the picture, I am able to see things and people CLEARLY, and recognize and avoid relationships that are doomed from the start. When a person sees that you are convicted and saving yourself for your mate, the potential suitor will either step up to the plate – or leave you alone. This way you don't waste too much time with men who have less than honorable intentions. Oh, they may test your resolve, but stand firm and you will truly know who is for you, and who is simply out for themselves. Not only that, you are ensuring your salvation, as well as your partner's, and also allowing yourself to get to know each other on a RELATIONSHIP level to see if you are evenly yoked. If so, then things can proceed naturally to marriage. If not, well perhaps you got in a good movie, or a nice dinner or two in the process - and perhaps a convert to Christ!

2.   **CONDUCT MYSELF AS A GODLY WOMAN**: Society's idea of 'The Strong Black Woman' is over-rated. What we need to be focusing on is what kind of woman does GOD want us to be? As it states in 1 Corinthians 11:3, ***"But I want you to know that the head of every man is Christ, the head of woman is man, and the head of Christ is God."*** Which means as he is to love and protect us women, we have to honor, obey and respect the man if he is living in love and obedience to Christ. We can't be going around calling men 'dogs', cussing them out and telling them they are no good, while we run rampant and try to dominate them in our relationships.

We are truly only strong if we uplift our men, respect them, take care of home and raise our children, and be their helpmate. They will respond in kind by WANTING to come home and be with us and their families, if they are TRULY Godly men. If a man wants to be with you, nothing will keep him from you. If you feel you have to search through his phone, repeatedly drive by his house, check up on him at work, rifle through his email or Facebook page to see if he's cheating on you, etc. – either he's not worth it or you're not ready for the relationship. Rather than pull your hair out, let it go and find a person deserving of what you have to offer, and work on yourself in the process. Mutual trust is a MUST in any relationship, be it a friend or a mate. We also have to conduct ourselves in a Godly manner by refraining from profanity, dressing modestly, and behaving maturely and respectfully towards all. **Proverbs 31:10-30**, as well as **Galatians 5:22-24** spell out very well how we are supposed to behave in Christ. We have to conform to God's ideal, NOT man's, and we will have our just reward – in His time, not ours.

3. **<u>LET GOD'S HOLY SPIRIT SHINE IN YOU FOR ALL TO SEE:</u>** God is Love. God's ways are not our ways and His thoughts are not our thoughts; His ways make no sense to the world, but they are essential for OUR very existence. To get Love, you must GIVE Love. To get money, you must GIVE your money – to help someone else. To solve your problems, help someone else solve THEIR problems. To receive blessings, you must GIVE of yourself to help another – in LOVE. That, in itself, is the greatest blessing of all – to be able to BLESS someone else in love, in God's name. There is no greater love than sacrifice of oneself to give to their friend **(John 15:13)** – and no greater blessing, for God will never leave us nor forsake us, His children. He sees all and will reward in kind – *"And my God shall supply all your need according to His riches in glory by Christ Jesus."* Philippians 4:19.

GLORY BE TO GOD!

SONG OF SOLOMON – HAVING SEX GOD'S WAY!

In the past 40+ years that I have been attending church, I must admit that it has only been since I have joined my present church home that the subject of sex has been brought up and discussed during services. Oh, it has been preached that people should refrain from having sex until they are married – that is 'understood' throughout the Christian community. Truth be told, many are NOT waiting until they are married to partake in the act, and to be honest, I believe it is partially the fault of the church for not explaining exactly WHY God wants us to save ourselves for marriage, nor how IMPORTANT it is to God to obey His word. Indeed scripture says, ***"Do you not know that the unrighteous will not inherit the kingdom of God? Do not be deceived. Neither fornicators, nor idolaters, nor adulterers, nor homosexuals, nor sodomites, nor thieves, nor covetous, nor drunkards, nor revilers, nor extortioners will inherit the kingdom of God." 1 Corinthians 6:9& 10.*** In other words, those who have sex before marriage, fornicators, will NOT inherit the kingdom of God!

Perhaps this miseducation is due to the fact that many churches either don't mention sex at all, or they shy away from teaching from the Song of Solomon because they don't know how to approach it. They may feel that they may in fact trigger even more sin in the church if they even mention the word 'sex' from the pulpit.

However, if you read and study the Song of Solomon, it will tell you WHY He ordains, even BLESSES, sex WITHIN the marriage bed. Of course, His order to "BE FRUITFUL AND MULTIPLY" (FOUND IN GENESIS 1:22 & 28) is always quick to come to mind, but God is also saying that there are more far-reaching things to be considered here.

First, there is the issue of what defines a marriage according to God – MARRIAGE IS THE COVENANT (PROMISE NOT TO BE BROKEN) UNION OF ONE MAN TO ONE WOMAN WITHIN THE BODY OF CHRIST (the covenant relationship is proven in MALACHI 2:14). And covenants are sealed in blood, the virgin bride's blood, once her 'seal' is broken! The first marriage was that of Adam and Eve, when God fashioned Eve from Adam's rib and made her his helpmate (GENESIS 1:21-25), ending with VERSE 25, "AND THEY WERE BOTH NAKED, THE MAN AND HIS WIFE, AND WERE NOT ASHAMED." This is how one knows that marriage is intended for a man and a woman – God created Adam and Eve, NOT Adam and Steve!!

Secondly, there is the matter of soul ties. A soul tie is the knitting together of two souls that can either bring tremendous blessings in a Godly relationship, or tremendous destruction when made between the wrong persons. A soul tie in the Bible can be described by the words 'knit', 'join' or 'cleave', meaning to bring closer together, or be attached to someone, as in adhere to one another like glue. The best examples of this is in GENESIS 2:24, "THEREFORE SHALL A MAN LEAVE HIS FATHER AND HIS MOTHER, AND SHALL CLEAVE UNTO HIS WIFE; AND THEY SHALL BE ONE FLESH," and EPHESIANS 5:31, "FOR THIS REASON A MAN SHALL LEAVE HIS FATHER AND MOTHER AND BE JOINED TO HIS WIFE, AND THE TWO SHALL BECOME ONE FLESH." Therefore, soul ties are meant for TWO people to be joined together as ONE flesh, one unit. Every time a man and a woman have sex, a soul tie is created – and this is another reason WHY sex is meant to be had between two MARRIED people, because these soul ties remain even if the couple stay together and marry, or whether it is a one-night stand. This is the reason why people who have multiple sex partners have problems ranging from just plain feeling empty inside after your sex partner goes home, being non-committal (why buy the cow if you can get the milk for free?), depression, unwanted pregnancies, 'baby mama drama', sexually transmitted diseases (including AIDS), dead-beat dads, etc. You get the picture...

Now those adults who are single and have children already, and/or are no longer virgins, do not despair – Simply REPENT and ask God to wash away your sins, and start from THIS POINT FORWARD to give your body and your life over to God, and begin anew! A celibate lifestyle may not be easy, but I tell you that God will allow you to see and read people easier and more quickly, thus avoiding the very SAME traps that can befall virgins, as stated above. It will also bring you a sense of peace, security and strength you never thought you could possess because your stress level will be MUCH lower, and you won't waste much time and emotions on doomed relationships, or worrying about unwanted pregnancies or disease.

Okay, now that we have these basic understandings down, let's explore probably the most interesting, intriguing and possibly misunderstood book in the Bible, Song of Solomon.

The Book Song of Solomon IS very poetic and the poet, credited to Solomon, is very skilled in his descriptions. It actually describes how two people, who are married, and are VIRGINS, are supposed to BE, FEEL and ACT as far as God is concerned. You see, there are THREE people who are speaking in this book: the Husband, the Wife, and GOD. It also shows how God blessed this union as SACRED, because He brought them together in marriage.

The groom's awesomeness and the wife's wanting is described by the bride for her husband, in her voice; *"LET HIM KISS ME WITH THE KISSES OF HIS MOUTH – FOR YOUR LOVE IS MORE DELIGHTFUL THAN WINE, PLEASING IS THE FRAGRANCE OF YOUR PERFUMES; YOUR NAME IS LIKE PERFUME POURED OUT. NO WONDER THE MAIDENS LOVE YOU! TAKE ME AWAY WITH YOU – LET US HURRY! LET THE KING BRING ME INTO HIS CHAMBERS," VERSES 1:2-4.* Also,

"LISTEN! MY LOVER! LOOK! HERE HE COMES, LEAPING ACROSS THE MOUNTAINS, BOUNDING OVER THE HILLS. MY LOVER IS LIKE A GAZELLE OR A YOUNG STAG. LOOK! THERE HE STANDS BEHIND OUR WALL, GAZING THROUGH THE WINDOWS, PEERING THROUGH THE LATTICE," VERSES 2:8-9.

The wife describes her young, handsome, and virile lover in the previous verses. There is much more as you continue reading, but she continues to express her love and admiration of her husband throughout the Book.

God's approving comments of her admiration is also apparent; *"WE REJOICE AND DELIGHT IN YOU; WE WILL PRAISE YOUR LOVE MORE THAN WINE," VERSE 1:4.*

She also admonishes young women to be modest, and not tempt the desires of men before true love is found; *"DAUGHTERS OF JERUSALEM, I CHARGE YOU BY THE GAZELLES AND BY THE DOES OF THE FIELD: DO NOT AROUSE OR AWAKEN LOVE UNTIL IT SO DESIRES," VERSE 3:5.* That is, for women to not dress provocatively, or behave in a way that would make men seek them sexually before they are given in marriage. This helps them remain chaste and be able to give themselves totally to their own husbands when God delivers him to them.

Now the husband then speaks and describes her beauty and his desire for her, with God's approving comments as well. *"HOW BEAUTIFUL YOU ARE MY DARLING! OH HOW BEAUTIFUL! YOUR EYES BEHIND YOUR VEIL ARE DOVES. YOUR HAIR IS LIKE A FLOCK OF GOATS DESCENDING FROM MOUNT GILEAD," VERSE 4:1.* Now he continues to describe how beautiful his bride is, and how luscious and tempting her body is, *"YOUR TWO BREASTS ARE LIKE TWO FAWNS, LIKE TWIN FAWNS OF A GAZELLE, THAT BROWSE AMONG THE LILIES," VERSE 4:5,* and continues the description of his journey downward.

However, line 4:12 proclaims, *"YOU ARE A GARDEN LOCKED UP, MY SISTER, MY BRIDE; YOU ARE A SPRING ENCLOSED, A SEALED FOUNTAIN",* meaning that the bride is a VIRGIN, with a 'treasure' that is to be known ONLY to the husband! He continues on, *"YOUR PLANTS ARE AN ORCHARD OF POMEGRANATES WITH CHOICE FRUITS, WITH HENNA AND NARD, NARD AND SAFFRON, CALAMUS AND CINNAMON WITH EVERY KIND OF INCENSE TREE, WITH MYRRH AND ALOES, AND ALL THE FINEST SPICES," VERSES 4:13-14.*

With the desires of both husband and wife mounting, she finally declares, *"LET MY LOVER COME INTO HIS GARDEN AND TASTE ITS CHOICE FRUITS," IN VERSE 4:16.* The husband states, *"I HAVE COME INTO MY GARDEN, MY SISTER, MY BRIDE, I HAVE GATHERED MY MYRRH WITH MY SPICE, I HAVE EATEN MY HONEYCOMB AND MY HONEY, I HAVE DRUNK MY WINE AND MY MILK."* The act of intercourse has since commenced, and God is pleased.

He gives His approval; *"EAT O FRIENDS, AND DRINK; DRINK YOUR FILL, O LOVERS!"* all in *VERSE 5:1.*

Now one might say that this Book is a love letter between husband and wife on their marriage bed, with which God is very well pleased. God has blessed this union because these lovers OBEYED His will and were righteous, and He then delivered to them the desires of their hearts. This is apparently true, but it goes a bit deeper than that.

Metaphorically speaking, as far as all Christians are concerned, Jesus is the Husband, and the Church is the Bride. This also describes now how Jesus sees us, His church, and once we are Raptured, He takes us, the Church, as His Bride! This Book also describes how much Jesus loves us, how He sees His church! Therefore marriage, and marital relations, is only a small preview of the JOY and ECSTASY, (which is represented by the human orgasm), we will feel when we are finally married to Christ!! This is only a small taste of what awaits us as His Church, Jesus' Bride! So in this sense, all marriages are a PREVIEW of what WE will have once we are joined with Christ; so you can ultimately say that Song of Solomon is God's love letter to US!

Many do not preach on it as such, but my Pastor does because over half of our congregation is under 30 years of age, with many adult singles as well. As a married man with 5 children, he is not only instructing the congregation, but also teaching his own children the importance of being obedient to God with their bodies. It helps us to understand how to please God and keep ourselves chaste until our mate comes along.

We need more Pastors to tackle this and teach this to the young and singles of their congregations. I believe this would pack a powerful punch, and ultimately reduce the incidences of sexual immorality among members of the Church - a BIG problem in society today.

We must always seek to honor God with our hearts, our souls and our minds, as instructed in the Great Commission, MATTHEW 22:37, *"YOU SHALL LOVE THE LORD YOUR GOD WITH ALL YOUR HEART, WITH ALL YOUR SOUL, AND WITH ALL YOUR MIND."* Do this, and your BODY will definitely follow! Also remember, *"SEEK FIRST THE KINGDOM OF GOD AND HIS RIGHTEOUSNESS, AND ALL THESE THINGS WILL BE ADDED UNTO YOU." MATTHEW 6:33.*

Glory be to God!

SPIRITUAL WARFARE

I really see that you are trying to be there for me...
and I am so tired of dealing with all this misery.
I can see the handwriting on the wall,
and all I want is to be loved and happy, that's all.

I will return the favor, I have lots of love to give,
but to the only man I will love for as long as I live.
For almost three long years I have saved myself for him
Promising God that I will not give it up on a whim.

I feel strongly for you, your words are drawing me near
the brink of telling my other friend to get the heck outta here
I won't give it to him because commitment is 'not his bag',
He tries to persuade me to fall, then he makes me feel sad.

I need someone who understands that love is not all in the act,
But comes from the heart and he can't understand that fact.
You must love me for my mind and my soul, be faithful and true,
I don't trust that in him, but I can see it in you...

Loyalty means a lot so I know what I must do.
It is hard for me to confront the burden I face, its true
Been with him awhile now but I'm tired of the fight

I just want to freely love someone with all of my might.

If this is you, then I know what I must do,

Can I place my trust, my life and my soul with you?

I sit and I cry, and I stare at these four walls,

Should I trust in you, and give you my self, my all?

I pray to God that He sent you to me

To be there for us, help me be all that I can be.

Because only in that circumstance will I truly know

That you are the One and only for my heart, my body, and my soul.

ADAM WAS A PUNK!!

Yes, I said it - Adam was a PUNK, the first BONA FIDE punk, and that's why sin entered this world. Lots of people blame Eve, but she was only the instrument satan used to try and get the world to follow him and NOT God – the buck stopped with Adam, and he PUNKED OUT!

For me to say all this, we must first start at the beginning... the VERY beginning.

"In the beginning, God created the heaven and the earth." *Genesis 1:1.* Through Genesis 1:2-25, the scriptures go on to say how the waters were formed, He declared, 'Let there be light', and there it was in the form of the sun, how the ground (firmament), grass, trees, the moon & stars, the fowl of the air and fish of the sea, creatures that roamed the earth, and how He made every creature after its own kind so they could reproduce, and how it was ALL good.

Now when God created the heaven, and before He created Adam, He also created beings, angels, as helpers to manage that which He was creating on earth. He created one that had almost all the strength and power that He Himself had, Lucifer, the most beautiful Angel, who was also a musician; music was originally created to praise God in the first place. The earth once before had form, but the earth was 'formless' (Genesis 1:2), and this formlessness was caused by Lucifer's earlier Fall from God's grace due to pride, and Lucifer's name was changed to satan (Ezekiel 28:13-18 and Isaiah 14:12-17). These scripture passages read:

*"**Thou has been in Eden the garden of God**; every precious stone was your covering the sardius, topaz, the diamond, the beryl, the onyx, the jasper, the sapphire the emerald and the carbuncle and gold; the workmanship of your tablets and of your pipes was prepared in you in the day that you were created. You are the anointed cherub that covereth; and I have set you so, you were upon the holy mountain of God; you have walked up and down in the midst of the stones of fire.*

Your heart was lifted up because of your beauty, you have corrupted your wisdom by reason of your brightness: I will cast you to the ground, I will lay you before kings, that they may behold you. You have defiled your sanctuaries by the multitude of your iniquities, by the iniquity of your traffick; therefore I will bring forth a fire from the midst of you, it shall devour you and I will bring you to ashes upon the earth in the sight of all those who behold you." **Here the scriptures confirm that Lucifer was in the garden of Eden before Adam and his wife were created. (Ezekiel 28:13-18).**

"How thou art fallen from heaven, O Lucifer, son of the morning; how art thou cut down to the ground, who did weaken the nations. For you have said in your heart, I will ascend into heaven, I will exalt my throne above the stars of God; I will sit also upon the mount of the congregation in the sides of the North; I will ascend above the heights of the clouds; I will be like the most High."

Here the scriptures confirm Lucifer's fall because of pride. And in rebellion, satan makes his plan to spite God. Note that satan cannot accomplish this without man - because man has redemption and free will. Satan does not. Angels do not have redemption. (Isaiah 14:12-17).

When satan was cast out of heaven, he took a legion of angels with him, a third of all the angels, who are now called demons – the fallen angels (Matthew 12:24; 25:41, Daniel 10:10-20; Matthew 10:1; Ephesians 6:12). This is how satan gets help trying to win souls to him, just as God instructs us through the Great Commission to win souls to the Lord.

Now let's get back to Genesis 1:26-27, which reads, *"And God said, Let us make man in our image, after our likeness: and let them have dominion over the fish of the sea, and over the fowl of the air, and over the cattle, and over all the earth, and over every creeping thing that creepeth upon the earth. So God created man in his own image, in the image of God he created him; male and female he created them."*

He then declared all His creations good and this all took six days. On the seventh day He blessed them all and then rested (Genesis 2:1-3).

The remainder of Genesis 2 details how God created Adam from the dust of the earth, and how He placed Adam in the Garden of Eden, for him to tend to it and be free to reign over the earth for Him. He CLEARLY instructed Adam, in verses 16-17, *"And the Lord commanded the man, saying, Of every tree of the garden thou mayest freely eat; But of the tree of the knowledge of good and evil, thou shalt not eat of it: for in the day that thou eatest thereof, thou shalt surely die."* This suggests that we were meant to live forever, NEVER to die. God then had Adam name each creature as they paraded by him, and this was done also to let Adam know how much he needed a helpmate as well. God declared that it was "not good that the man should be alone" in verse 18, and in verses 21-25, God describes how he put Adam in a deep sleep, formed Eve, his helpmate, from his rib (not from the top of his head to be over him, nor from his feet to be beneath him, but from his side to be his equal helpmate). So now we have the model of ONE husband to ONE wife, the Biblical model of marriage, from the very beginning, *"And Adam said, This is now bone of my bone, flesh of my flesh: she shall be called Woman, because she was taken out of Man. Therefore shall a man leave his father and his mother, and shall cleave unto his wife; and they shall be one flesh. And they were both naked, the man and his wife, and were not ashamed."* Keep in mind they were created HOLY, without sin, which means that if they were in His image, they also had God's shekinah glory about them, and of course they were not ashamed.

Now with all this being said and understood, this is where things REALLY get interesting.

Before the creation of Woman, Lucifer was God's greatest creation – he was (and still is) perfect in beauty, and is still the greatest of musicians. He has NOT changed in his appearance or abilities, only his worship to God has changed – satan wants us to worship him INSTEAD of God because of his PRIDE – he wants to be in control of all in this world, and he can only touch us if God allows it.

But now, Woman is in the picture – and SHE surpasses satan in beauty, challenges his intelligence, and in the ability to multi-task, and do many things that satan considers a challenge to his authority. WOMAN is God's GREATEST creation now – she took satan's place, and he is jealous! So now he devises a plan to bring down God's perfect world – using God's greatest creation, WOMAN!

Look at what happens once we get to Genesis 3:1-5; satan, disguised as the serpent, engages in conversation with Eve, suggesting to her that she will 'surely not die' if she eats of the forbidden fruit from the tree of the knowledge of good and evil. She explains that they can eat everything else, just not of that tree, meaning that Adam has ALREADY explained to her what God told him. The serpent finally persuades her to eat, and she does, and just as the serpent said, nothing happened – yet. But the KEY VERSE is Genesis 3:6, which reads:

"And when the woman saw that the tree was good for food, and that it was pleasant to the eyes, and a tree to be desired to make one wise, she took of the fruit thereof, and did eat, and gave also unto her husband with her; and he did eat."

Now , this suggests that Adam was **standing there WITH HER** while the serpent talked to her, persuaded her to eat, and she turned to 'her husband with her', who then ate of the fruit also.

WHAT?!?!?   Picture this, especially the MEN out there...

You and your woman are out on the town, minding your own business, and this slick-talking dude tries to rap to your woman in front of your face! He's rapping to her, even offering her a piece of fruit right **in front of you!!** And not only do you let her rap to this guy, but you not only **LET HER** take some of this guy's fruit, but **YOU** eat it also, only to find it's POISON – it's gonna kill you both, AFTER you have already been warned b your father **NOT** to take fruit from strangers! Is this not the idea of a **PUNK** to YOU???

Wouldn't YOU be considered a PUNK if you let some guy try and rap to your woman and **you Not** stand up to him and tell him to get lost, if not go further and punch his lights out??

ADAM GOT **PUNKED** BY SATAN, AND HE USED A WOMAN, A BEING *SUPERIOR* TO HIM, TO DO IT!

Sin entered the world because Adam did not stand up to the serpent, and heed God's command to NOT eat that fruit! There is a divine order established by God that we live by - God is the head of Jesus, who is the head of Man, who is the head of Woman. Even though Eve ate, it was Adam's job to stop the serpent AND her, because God gave the command to **WHO??** He gave it to the **MAN**, He gave it to Adam, who covered Eve's sins as long as he obeyed God and His commands – but with the failure of Adam, we are now ALL beings that not only will one day perish (unless we repent and give our lives over to Jesus, Who was God in the flesh, sent to die for our sins and **DEFEATED** death, our only source of salvation). The consequences of Eve's sin is for women to bear pain in childbirth; all of which is spelled out in the remainder of Genesis 3. Verse 7 continues, *"And the eyes of both were opened, and they knew that they were naked; and they sewed fig leaves together, and made themselves aprons."*

First, they were not ashamed because they were made in God's image, and the shekinah glory covered them... But as soon as Adam ate, sin entered the world, and their shekinah glory *VANISHED*, and they were there, bare and naked, and shame came upon them because the **IMMEDIATELY** knew something was dreadfully wrong – God admonishes them for their grave error in the rest of Genesis 3, and pours out His wrath & judgment where God thrust out Adam and Eve, where they were to live forever, and installed cherubim with a sword of fire to protect the tree from here on out (Genesis 3:8-24).

So let this be a CLEAR INDICATION to all, especially to MEN, to lead your lives and guide your families as GOD COMMANDS in His Word, lest YOU be the next PUNK God has to deal with!

Peace & Blessings to you all...

Michele Green, aka RM Green -

LOVE IS.....

Turning a frown into a smile,

Or a tear into a hug,

Visiting for a long while,

A chill warmed by hot chocolate in a mug.

Deep conversations lasting for hours,

Encouragement when fear rears it's ugly head.

A tender clasp with hands full of flowers,

While gazing adoringly and speechless from the bed.

Sage advice given from the heart,

Teaching each other life lessons learned.

Sharing passions and future plans to start

Mutually enjoying each one's talent and respect earned.

A child's touch that pierces the soul,

Guiding new beings to maturity, then setting free

Eyes of sheer wonderment that babies behold,

When grown, holding keys to the future they see.

Romantic kisses and passionate embraces,

Experiencing the ultimate in physical bliss.

Exploring each other's secret places

And when apart, each other's essence is sorely missed.

Seeking God and following in His walk

Searching for truth and obeying His divine Word.

Allowing His light to shine in how we act and talk

Together forever, bound for life, His Will be heard.

WHY DOESN'T GOD ANSWER MY PRAYERS?

I am sure at one time or another we have all asked ourselves this same question many times over. You find yourself in a situation and have prayed about it, and it seems that God is nowhere in sight. Even those of us Christians who have been in the Word for years have asked themselves, *'Why isn't God answering my prayers?'*

Truth be told, in many cases we will find that He HAS answered your prayers, just not in the way YOU wanted or expected!

God answers our prayers in one of three ways; **YES, NO and WAIT**. That is the way He has always done it and will always do so. He can answer your prayers immediately, or He can tell you NO, or He can say – WAIT, He is going before you do handle some things, OR He has some work to do on YOU, (or YOU have some work to do on you), THEN you can have it.

"For I am the Lord, I change not; therefore ye sons of Jacob are not consumed." Malachi 3:6. The Lord Jesus also stated, in *Matthew 24:35, "Heaven and earth shall pass away, but my words shall not pass away."* Therefore, not only does God NOT change – we must conform to Him, He does NOT conform to us – but His Word is the absolute TRUTH, and will remain so until the end of time.

According to Scripture, we have some responsibilities to live up to if we expect God to listen to and/or answer our prayers. In the Bible studies we have had at my church our Pastor has often referred to the proper order of prayer (which the Lord's Prayer also reflects), is reflected in the acronym **ACTS: A- Adoration (Praise), C-Confession (of our sins),T- Thanksgiving (thanking Him for all the blessings He has bestowed upon you; and S-Supplication (asking for what you need in prayer).**

PRAYER IS NOT FOR SHOW – *"And when you pray, you shall not be like the hypocrites. For they love to pray standing in the synagogues and on the corners of the streets, that they may be seen by men. Assuredly, I say to you, they have their reward. But you, when you pray, go into your room, and when you have shut your door, pray to your Father Who is in the secret place; and your Father, Who sees in secret, will reward you openly. Therefore, do not be like them. For your Father knows the things you have need of before you ask Him." Matthew 6:5-8.* Prayer is one-on-one communication with God. The Lord's Prayer follows this passage in verses 9-13, and Jesus is teaching His disciples HOW to pray in this entire passage.   Who better to teach you how to pray than Jesus?

BELIEVERS SHOULD LIVE IN A SPIRIT OF PRAYER – *"Pray without ceasing." 1 Thessalonians 5:17.* We should be living so that we are in tune with God at all times – and as things arise during the day, be prayerful for whatever you are calling upon God for – much like your friend, because God IS our closest Friend – and talk to Him the same way you would talk with a friend. He WANTS a PERSONAL relationship with EACH of us, and the Holy Spirit will always guide us if we continue to *"SEEK FIRST the kingdom of GOD and His righteousness, and all these things shall be added unto you." – Matthew 6:33.*

PRAYERS OF A RIGHTEOUS PERSON MAKE A DIFFERENCE – *"Confess your trespasses to one another, and pray for one another, that you will be healed. The effective, fervent prayer of a righteous man avails much." James 5:16.* So, the question is, Ladies & Gentlemen, **HOW YOU LIVIN'?** If you are living according to God's Word and seek Him with your heart, God calls your prayers *'fervent and effective'*, meaning that He must answer them. However, if you are living in the ways of the world and are not even trying to live up to His standards, then don't expect many of your prayers to be answered. WE conform to Him, God does NOT conform to US! Sin builds barriers between us and God.

This is something I confess I have been guilty of for much of my life, rationalizing away sinful behavior, believing that God will forgive me if I do something (such as telling 'little white lies'; having sex without being married; taking pens, paper, binders, etc. home from work with permission, which is stealing!) because I was doing it for a 'good' purpose, or I was not 'hurting' anyone – what I did NOT want to admit was that each one of those acts were behaviors FORBIDDEN by God, and each time I did them I was hurting GOD!! It is true that we all have within us a sin nature, so even though we cannot do it perfectly, we should always strive to do better - and this should come from the HEART to please God, NOT just because you want your prayers answered. One cannot **intentionally** do wrong – or sin – WITHOUT hurting God! Would YOU bless someone who was HURTING you?   Think about it...

GOD EXPECTS US TO PRAY AND FAST – *"And Jesus said unto them, 'Can the children of the bridechamber fast, while the bridegroom is with them? As long as they have the bridegroom with them, they cannot fast. But the days will come, when the bridegroom shall be taken away from them, and then they shall fast in those days." Mark 2:19-20.* There are many references to prayer and fasting throughout the Bible, and are also found in the Old Testament, for example, Isaiah 58:1-8. It was always customary and EXPECTED to not only pray, but FAST to have God hear our prayers. What my Pastor explains Jesus is saying in Mark 2:19-20 is that while the disciples – and indeed the people (his bride, the 'church') - had Him there in their presence, they didn't fast because He was there with them to teach them and give them what they need.

However, once He was gone from them, they needed to pray as well as fast – sacrifice something of themselves – in order to stay close to Him. The blood of animals is no longer be sacrificed to cover sins – Jesus was sacrificed and His blood now covers all our sins, but we now must sacrifice something – fast for Him, to show Him our love and devotion. Jesus paid the ULTIMATE price for us... what will YOU sacrifice for Him?

Most times, fasting tends to involve food, which is mainly what was referred to in the Bible. But fasting is NOT limited to food – it is the VOLUNTARY denial of something YOU hold as important or dear to YOU that you sacrifice in order to show your love and devotion to God. It may be FOOD, or TV, or COMPUTER, or CELLPHONE (and don't choose your cellphone because you haven't paid the bill and it's off anyway!!), etc. - ANYTHING you hold in HIGH REGARD that you give up temporarily for God, will suffice. And God KNOWS your heart, so don't think you are fooling Him – or will EVER fool Him, because you're NOT! GOD knows you better than you know yourself, down to the very number of hairs on your head. So the question remains... **What are YOU willing to SACRIFICE for GOD???**

Sometimes, if we sit back and take a hard look at ourselves, we know or discover what our problems are and what needs to be changed in our lives. This study here speaks to me as much as I pray it will speak to you, as God laid it on my heart to share this. *Peace & Blessings, and May God Bless you ALL!*

SEEK THE ONE

You are like a mighty rock
Perched up high against the endless sky
Pillar of strength, and noble of character
Giving support to the weak, steadfast by and by.

Your children depend on you
To love them, teach them, show them every day
How to mature into noble men, full of strength
Fair to all, until their own maturity leads their way.

Your family needs your shoulder to lean on,
Favors to be done, unceasing by decree
Friends ask your help, guidance and advice
Someone to talk to, laugh with and be free.

The weight of the world is upon your shoulders,
Crushing down your spirit, withering at your feet.
Release from these burdens is what you seek
Before they destroy your soul, and you fall down in defeat.

Taking care of so many
Is a responsibility placed on a select few
But after tending the needs of so many,
Who is taking care of YOU?

When it seems the world needs you
Only for what it can use and take from you,
Rest assured there is ONE out there
Who only wants to GIVE, only and truly for you...

GIVE you JOY when your heart is broken,
GIVE you PEACE when turmoil abounds,
GIVE you HAPPINESS when your spirit is heavy,
GIVE you LOVE, when the world seems so cold.

SEEK THE ONE - JESUS, and your troubles will be..

Done.

JUDGE NOT, LEST YOU BE JUDGED!

There is hardly a verse in the Bible that has been misused by mere men and ministers alike, *"Judge not, that you be not judged." Matthew 7:1.* In the past, I have even used this phrase myself to justify thoughts and behaviors not in keeping with societal, or even Godly, standards. Therefore I am teaching myself, as well as sharing with you, my friends, this same lesson. Been there and done that!

Many times when a verse in the Bible is spit out as much as this one is, it is often taken out of context so that the person speaking it can use it to their advantage, to champion and/or justify whatever belief or action they are taking. I have done it many times myself, so I know from which perspective I speak. But we must take this verse and read the WHOLE account before we can make any kind of statement as to what is meant by it. The remainder of this passage reads as follows;

"For with what judgment you judge, you will be judged; and with the measure you use, it will be measured back to you. And why do you look at the speck in your brother's eye, but do not consider the plank in your own eye? Or how can you say to your brother, 'Let me remove the speck from your eye'; and look, a plank is in your own eye? Hypocrite! First remove the plank from your own eye, and then you will see clearly to remove the speck from your brother's eye." Matthew 7:2-5.

We had Bible study on this very verse, and Pastor clearly explained that Jesus was NOT saying that we should NOT judge, but we should not judge others when we are guilty of the same offense. That is like being a parent who smokes and tries to teach their children to NOT smoke! The kids look at you like you are crazy! Why do you tell us not to do what you do so openly? That is being a hypocrite.... the parent could very well not want the children to become smokers such as they are for health reasons, but we must show by EXAMPLE. When we judge, we should judge RIGHTEOUSLY, and to win our brother/sister back to Christ.

Actually, we are COMMANDED by God to approach that brother or sister one on one, with love, that they may see the error of their ways and turn back to God, *""If your brother sins, go and show him his fault in private; if he listens to you, you have won your brother. But if he does not listen to you, take one or two more with you, so that BY THE MOUTH OF TWO OR THREE WITNESSES EVERY FACT MAY BE CONFIRMED. If he refuses to listen to them, tell it to the church; and if he refuses to listen even to the church, let him be to you as a Gentile and a tax collector," (Matthew 18:15-17).*

God EXPECTS us to right our brothers/sisters when they are clearly sinning against God, and their sin may infest the remainder of the flock (congregation) if it is NOT addressed and corrected, *"Do not judge by appearances, but judge with right judgment." (John 7:24).* So then, we are sometimes CALLED UPON to judge! For example, if you have a brother or sister who is shacking (living together with another without the benefit of marriage), and NO ONE says anything about it, they will then think that behavior is OK with God, and then other members of the church will begin to do it - *"A little leaven leavens the whole lump" (Galatians 5:9).*

If someone is doing wrong and you know it and do NOT admonish them, then YOU are just as guilty as permitting the sin to continue, or condoning it. DON'T judge the other person for having an extramarital affair if YOU'RE having an affair too! You have to fix YOURSELF BEFORE you can fix your brother/sister. However, if you are NOT guilty of the sin though, you not only have every RIGHT to admonish your brother/sister, you MUST in order to save them from their sin and clear YOUR name before God. To sit in silence and watch without saying or doing anything is condoning the sin. Just as if you WATCH someone hurt another and you refuse to get help for them... If they DIE because they didn't get needed medical treatment, it's just as if you murdered them because you could have called police or an ambulance and saved their life, but didn't. Same context..

We must conform to God's ways; He does not conform to US! And he does NOT regard our feelings when it comes to His laws... we either obey God or we don't! We are either on His side or not! *"For there is no respect of persons with God," Romans 2:11.* He treats us ALL the same, regardless of who we are, and we are not to be lukewarm either, or straddle the fence, with God. We are either HOT for Him, or we are satan's own by default. A lukewarm Christian sickens God, *"So then, because you are lukewarm, and neither cold nor hot, I will vomit you out my mouth," Revelation 3:16.*

I am HOT for my Lord and Savior, so this is why I went into all this to help my Christian brothers & sisters so that they may be blessed! I love you all, and may God continue to bless you all... ♥

"I can do ALL THINGS through Christ, Who strengthens me." Philippians 4:13.

A SPARROW'S MAJESTY

Hardly I breathe! Hardly do I breathe
Leaves on that rotted oak tree soon leave
Breezes in spring capture all beautiful scenes
I seen a sparrow in a thought shaded with 'dream'
Such a 'beautiful' it sing like Billie Holiday
Resting on hope and strange fruit- it sings
Pharaohs' musicians strings sullen melodies
As sparrows fly by looking down to that 'king

A sight so 'beautiful' and lovely as that 'king'
Would soon be torn and shorn for thee,
Wings that bear up what angels sing
For all the world be known what was done for me.
Land that rumbles with a thunderous shake
Earth torn apart, figures emerge and wander
What the eyes can see from that wondrous quake
'Tis too awesome to behold, too precious to squander.

SPEAKING IN TONGUES; *Say What?*

Until very recent years, I have spent a good part of my life attending church, sometimes visiting other churches. Quite frankly, for most of those years I have felt 'inadequate', or for lack of a better term, not 'spiritual' enough because many of the people in these churches 'spoke in tongues', and often 'fell out' in the pews in 'trances', muttering things that were unintelligible to me, who all appeared quite spiritual and sincere in their worship. Watching these incidents occur in the churches over the years left me thinking that perhaps I was not "spiritual' enough, or not loved by God enough, because I have honestly never been moved to either 'fall out' or 'speak in tongues', as other members of these congregations have. I have even been told that unless I spoke in tongues, I was not 'spiritual enough' to be able to communicate with God. All my life, and to this day, I have always been more of a calm presence, an 'observer', so that I can learn more about what God has to say so that I may apply it to my life, and have my life be more acceptable to Him.

During a recent Bible study, my Pastor finally put to rest all those thoughts of spiritual inadequacy I had been harboring all these years. The Bible CLEARLY states what is meant by 'speaking in tongues' in the New Testament book of Acts (which, by the way, is the ONLY book in the Bible where this has occurred) in chapters 2, 10 and 19.

<u>All of Acts Chapter 2</u> describes what happened at Pentecost, when Jews, as well as Gentiles, from other nations, were converted because as Peter and the other disciples preached, a great wind fell across them and enabled those who did not UNDERSTAND the NATIVE language the disciples WERE SPEAKING IN, they STILL UNDERSTOOD what was SAID as if they were speaking in the LISTENERS' native language, so that more than 3,000 were converted and baptized that day, and more in days to come. They were amazed and confused that they could understand all that was said, even though it spoken in the disciples OWN native language.

When someone commented that it couldn't possibly happen, that they were all drunk, Peter set them all straight in **Acts 2:14-40**. However, it is due to this Biblical occurrence that it is clear that GOD ACTED, so that people of ALL nations, Jews and Gentiles, could understand the gospel and be SAVED by it, as God intended. This was done so that as the gospel of Jesus was spread throughout the nations at Pentecost, LANGUAGE would not be a barrier!

In Acts Chapter 10, Peter shares the gospel of Jesus with Cornelius, who was a Gentile, a Roman and a soldier. Peter did NOT want to share the gospel of salvation with Cornelius because these Roman soldiers are the very ones PERSECUTING the Jews, but Peter obeyed God and went with Cornelius. God knew Cornelius was devoted to Him and feared Him, and Peter shared the gospel with those meeting in his home and they all became believers. They spoke with each other about it in THEIR OWN native languages, and understood, and it was then that Peter really knew and believed they were all saved. God had AGAIN revealed Himself so that all could UNDERSTAND His Word and the message of salvation and be SAVED, even though Peter spoke in his OWN native tongue. It has now really become clear to Peter that *'God does not show favoritism, but accepts men from every nation who fear Him and do what is right."* Acts 10:34-35.

Acts Chapter 19:1-7, the same type of occurrence happened that occurred at Pentecost. Paul went to preach in the church at Ephesus when it was learned that they had not yet accepted Christ in their hearts. Paul preached, and the followers heard the Word in their various languages and understood, because the Holy Ghost had come over them, and accepted the gospel of Jesus and salvation into their lives.

Now in **1 Corinthians 14**, Paul confronted the church in Corinth on several issues, INCLUDING the problem of using 'unknown tongues' in the church. Paul lays out some very specific rules regarding speaking in tongues in this chapter of the Bible, which also specifically calls for 'orderly worship', **(verse 14:40)**; *'But everything should be done in a fitting and orderly way'.*

The main lessons being taught by Paul is that many wish to receive the spiritual gifts of prophesy and tongues, but these 'tongues' should be a known language within the church setting so that EVERYONE who is in attendance can understand what is being said. *"But in the church, I would rather speak five intelligible words to instruct others, than ten thousand words in a tongue." (verse 14:19).* Paul states that if you do indeed speak in a tongue known only to you and God, it edifies YOU, not those around you, because they cannot understand you. To edify those around you, in church, one must speak in their language or have an interpreter so that ALL can know and understand God's word, and have the chance to be saved (**verses 14:1-6 & 26-40**). These are the guidelines that should be followed so that ALL in the congregation come away understanding what is being taught and said, and be given the chance to convert and follow Christ.

I encourage all to read all of the Chapters and Verses pointed out, preferably with a study Bible or Concordance, so you get the full picture of what was going on at the time, and receive the full understanding on your own, and come to your own conclusions. Study for yourself to know what God approves of, **2 Timothy 2:15**.

Consider this: Jesus NEVER spoke in tongues, nor has He required it of His believers. Think of it this way... Why should God give us a 'new tongue', when we often DO NOT use the language we are already fluent in to praise Him, or share Him with our neighbor? This gift of the Pentecost was given in the early church so that OTHERS who DID NOT know about Him, from other nations, could learn of Him, understand and have the chance to choose to follow Him and be saved. If you and God have a private language with which you communicate, as it is with many sets of twins or close siblings, that is wonderful and you should continue with your private communications with God – in private. But that is NOT for the Church, as God wishes ALL to understand the message being preached, which makes ALL the sense in the world to me.

This essay may not be popular with some, but being popular is NOT my intent – my intention is to be BIBLICAL, and to speak the truth as to what the Bible states. I also do this to carry out God's command in The Great Commission: Matthew 22:37-40, *"'You shall love the Lord your God with all your heart, with all your soul and with all your mind'. This is the first and Great Commandment. And the second is like it: 'You shall love your neighbor as yourself. On these two commandments hang all the law and the prophets.'"*

DO YOU HAVE AN ATTITUDE OF SERVITUDE TO GOD?

"You have heard that it was said, 'You shall love your neighbor and hate your enemy.' But I say to you, love your enemies, bless those who curse you, do good to those who hate you, and pray for those who spitefully use use you and persecute you, that you may be sons of your Father in Heaven; for He makes His sun rise on the evil and on the good, and sends rain on the just and on the unjust. For if you love those who love you, what reward have you? Do not even the tax collectors do the same? And if you greet your brethren only, what do you do more tan others? Do not even the tax collectors do so? Therefore you shall be perfect, just as your Father in Heaven is perfect." Matthew 5:43-48.

These are often hard words to hear, but even harder to do. God calls us to be set apart from the world - the world doesn't understand us, our thoughts and our actions, and we should not be doing what the world dictates we do. But if we just react in the natural, our feelings and emotions, we will be reacting as the world does, and this is not in keeping with what Christ says we should be. If someone hurts or murders your child, you instinctively want to hurt and/or murder them! Yet and still, there are people out there who FORGIVE the murderers of their children. HOW CAN THEY DO THAT? By holding on to God's love. Why? Because the hate actually festers inside of us and destroys US. In order to be free, they have to let the anger and hate go, so that THEY can free themselves of the anger and hurt and move on with their own lives, and God can use them to be a blessing to OTHERS. I know about this first hand, and it IS a freeing feeling to be able to forgive the person who hurt my own child, and then be able to be used by God to bless others. By no means is it EASY - it usually takes much time, prayer and fasting to bring these feelings to rest, but God WILL in time bring you to peace in His love. What a WONDERFUL and FREEING feeling it is to be USEFUL to our Lord!

Now this does NOT mean that the CONSEQUENCES for their wrong actions should, or will, be taken away. God is the Perfect Parent, and as we sin we sometimes have to bear the consequences for that sin. His Grace simply means that we do not automatically DIE on the spot for our sins; He will punish us at times and give us time to GET IT RIGHT before we come to His final judgment. We always reap what we sow, be it good fruit or bad fruit; **"Do not be deceived, God is not mocked; for whatever a man sows, that he will also reap. For he who sows to his flesh will of the flesh reap corruption, but he who sows to the Spirit will of the Spirit reap everlasting life. And let us not grow weary while doing good, for in due season we shall reap if we do not lose heart." Galatians 6:7-9.** Therefore if you break the law, the person upon whom you committed a crime may forgive you, but you may still have to face a prison sentence; if you have an extramarital affair your spouse may forgive you, but a child may be produced of that affair that you may have to care for and raise. Conversely, if you sow money into your education and work hard, it will produce a college degree that you can use to better your life, and that of your family. See how that works? You will ALWAYS reap whatever you sow, MORE than you sow, and LATER than you sow... that's God's Law!

This also means that you must also 'stop the hemorrhage' of the fruits of your blessings from going to waste. Suppose you are sowing your money into a cause that has been found to be squandering their money, such as a food bank where they are supposed to be feeding the hungry, but the larger portion of the money is actually going into the pockets of the organizers? Then **STOP GIVING** to that cause until you find another that uses its funds to actually give to the needy, where it belongs, so the fruits of your blessings are not wasted on those unfitting of God's, or your, plans.

When we pray, we are always asking for blessings, and over 90% of the time, these blessings are for US - personal blessings. Lord, I ask that You bless me with a new car; bless me with a new house; bless me with more money; bless me with a better job... Bless me, bless me, bless me.

Nothing wrong with asking for blessings, we are SUPPOSED to ask Him for the things we need and sometimes want. But how many times do you USE the blessings He bestows upon you for someone ELSE? Many times, God blesses us with things so that we can USE these things to BE a blessing to SOMEONE ELSE. When you get that new car, how many people did you contact and ask if they needed a ride anywhere (without the INTENT of just showing off your car - remember God reads our HEARTS)? When you got that new house, how many people did you find that needed a place to sleep did you invite in? When you got that new job, how many hungry children did you feed because you now had the funds to do so? Or how many elderly people did you buy groceries for so they could afford to buy the medication they needed in order to survive? God blesses you EVERY TIME He opens your eyes in the morning, but how many times have you awakened and said, "Wow God just blessed me with another day - I can't WAIT to bless SOMEONE ELSE today!"? I know I find myself GUILTY of this... I very rarely wake up EAGER to bless someone else that day, except perhaps on a birthday or special occasion. How about YOU?

God blesses US to BE a blessing to others, and many times we are limited in our blessings because we are SELFISH ourselves. Why would God bless you with MORE if you won't use your blessings to further bless another? Many times we block our OWN blessings this way. **"And God is able to make all grace abound toward you, that you, always having sufficiency in all things, may have an abundance for every good work. As it is written: 'He dispensed abroad, He has given to the poor, His righteousness endures forever.' Now may He who supplies seed to the sower, and bread for food, supply and multiply the seed you have sown and increase the fruits of your righteousness, while you are enriched in everything for all liberality, which causes thanksgiving through us to God. For the administration of this service not only supplies the needs of the saints, but also is abounding through many thanksgivings to God, while, through the proof of this ministry,**

they glorify God for the obedience of your confession to the gospel of Christ, and for your liberal sharing with them and all men, and by their prayer for you, who long for you because of the exceeding grace of God in you." 2 Corinthians 9:8-14. We are of course allowed to enjoy our blessings, but the MAIN reason God blesses us is so that we can BE a blessing to OTHERS, and that is the attitude of servitude we need to have in order to please God.

Jesus healed EVERYONE, Jew and Gentile, in His days here on earth. He even served his own Apostles and washed their feet. Should we not follow His own example? If we seek to be great, we need to be followers FIRST, we need to be servants FIRST, and in our obedience He will be there along the way to making US great servants for Him! **"Remember the word that I said to you, 'A servant is not greater than his master.' If they persecuted Me, they will also persecute you. If they kept My word, they will keep yours also." John 15:20.** Joseph is one such example... he was persecuted by his jealous brothers and thrown into slavery to the Pharaoh, and years later was exhalted to be his second in command, and actually saved those same brothers, and his father, from death in the coming famine. Joseph blessed them, even though he had every right to persecute them for what they did to him. That was his faith in God, and his attitude of servitude, that had him forgive and actually SAVE them from death! **(Read Genesis, Chapters 37 - 50).** Let's not grieve Jesus and crucify Him all over again anymore, but let's aspire to His goodness and greatness!

May God be there with you on your road to SERVITUDE, to GREATNESS! In Jesus' name I pray.... Amen!

ABOUT THE AUTHOR

Born in New York City and raised in Brooklyn, NY and Roosevelt LI, NY, she began writing about 20+ years ago, writing primarily short stories for young adults. These stories depicted social ills that bothered her, such as homelessness, HIV and domestic abuse for starters. She attempted to get her stories published, but after about 200 attempts with no promises in sight, became discouraged and quit writing for about 14 years.

When her grandmother died in February, 2006, the lesson her death seemed to be teaching her is that if you have a dream, you had better realize it now before it is too late. She always had a dream of publishing a novel, but the first thing she did was pen a poem to her grandmother, **'MY HEART'S SONG,** through tears of grief. That poem opened the floodgates to her writing career. And she's been going strong ever since.

In **August 2007**, she produced her first book, an anthology called **'THE PASSION WITHIN',** with five other writer friends, and she formed her own publishing company, **SAFE HAVEN PUBLISHING COMPANY**, primarily to learn about the publishing business and to produce her own works.

In April, 2008, she opened the company to accept outside authors and has now realized her dream of being an author and publisher. Her next novel, **'SHE COULD HEAR THE SILENCE'** is scheduled to be released by the company in 2013.

She also edited the book, **'A JOURNEY TO WELLNESS: A Series of Collective Thoughts'** by Debra D. Griffin, a book which chronicles Ms. Griffin's fight against breast cancer in words and pictures in 2007.

Also in **August, 2007**, she began broadcasting her own radio show, **AUTHOR SPEAK**, where she interviews authors about their lives, passions, inspiration to write, and their projects. You can find the archives or tune in live to her program at **www.The1EssenceRadio.com** . She is also the Assistant Station Manager of The1Essence Radio.

Ms. Green, now divorced, resides in Beaufort, SC and is the mother of three beautiful daughters and the new grandmother of her first granddaughter.